CRUISE FACTS

TRUTH & TIPS ABOUT CRUISE TRAVEL

KEN ROSSIGNOL

CRUISE FACTS

WHERE SHOULD WE SEND YOUR
STARTER LIBRARY?

ThePrivateerClause.com

Ken@ThePrivateerClause.com

KEN ROSSIGNOL

Tell me where to send your free book and a chance to win a FREE PAPERWHITE

GET ANOTHER BOOK FREE

Available in paperback and Audible at Amazon and retailers worldwide

The Marsha & Danny Jones Thrillers

1 The Privateer Clause
#2 Return of the Sea Empress
#3 Follow Titanic
#4 Follow Triangle – Vanish!
#5 Cruise Killer

CRUISE FACTS
#5 Beheaded – Terror By Land, Sea & Air

SIX KILLER THRILLER NOVELS - Marsha & Danny Jones Thriller Series Books 1 - 6

Additional books by Ken Rossignol

Chesapeake 1850

Chesapeake 1880

Chesapeake 1910 (coming soon)

Battle of Solomon's Island

KEN ROSSIGNOL

Titanic Series

Titanic 1912

Titanic & Lusitania- Survivor Stories (with Bruce M. Caplan)

Titanic Poetry, Music & Stories

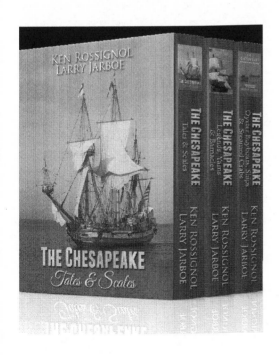

CRUISE FACTS

The Chesapeake: Tales Trio – The box set of all three of The Chesapeake series

The Chesapeake Series

The Chesapeake: Tales & Scales (with Larry Jarboe)

The Chesapeake: Legends, Yarns & Barnacles (with Larry Jarboe)

The Chesapeake: Oyster Buyboats, Ships & Steamed Crabs

Non-fiction

KLAN: Killing America

Panama 1914

The Story of The Rag

Leopold & Loeb Killed Bobby Franks (with Bruce M. Caplan)

Wreck of the Whale Ship Essex - Illustrated - NARRATIVE OF THE MOST EXTRAORDINARY AND DISTRESSING SHIPWRECK OF THE WHALE-SHIP ESSEX: Original News Stories of Whale Attacks & Cannibals

CHESAPEAKE CRIME CONFIDENTIAL

Coke Air: Chesapeake Crime Confidential

PIRACY and PIRATES – Non-fiction

Pirate Trials: Dastardly Deeds & Last Words

Pirate Trials: Hung by the Neck Until Dead

KEN ROSSIGNOL

Pirate Trials: Famous Murderous Pirates Book Series: THE LIVES AND ADVENTURES of FAMOUS and SUNDRY PIRATES

PIRATE TRIALS: The Three Pirates - Famous Murderous Pirate Books Series: The Islet of the Virgin

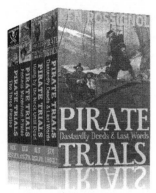

Four Pirate Novels of Murder, Executions, Romance & Treasure - Pirate Trials Series Books 1 - 4

Travel

Fire Cruise

Cruising the Waterfront Restaurants of the Potomac

Cruise Facts

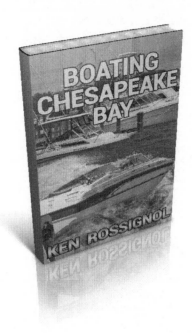

The Traveling Cheapskate series:

CRUISE FACTS

By Ken Rossignol

Contents

Chapter One

What to Expect

Are you thinking about joining the twenty-three million people who take a voyage on a cruise ship each year?

There are plenty of guides and books that feature all manner of advice, and most of them are likely good sources of information.

One of the best pieces of advice I have ever seen was this: "When preparing for travel, lay out all the clothes and all the money you expect you'll need. Then, take half the clothes and twice the money!"

Another priceless admonition was this: "There are two forms of travel – First Class and with children!"

Enough with the old jokes.

I often have folks on ships ask me, as if I am some sort of authority, what cruise line is the best. I really wouldn't know as I have been on many ships of various lines, and all I have observed is that every single one of them attempts to provide an excellent vacation for their passengers. Some, of course, have better luck at it than others.

However, I consider each cruise to be a rollicking success as long as the ship doesn't catch fire or capsize. With a thousand ships on the high seas, and all of them busy nearly every day of the year there are so few such incidents that it makes it really easy for the media to wring every last video clip out of the high-profile disasters.

Aside from being on one of those cruises, it is likely your first trip will be something you will remember for the rest of your life. I know, that British guy will soon starting painting his name on the side of the ship. He announced plans for a Virgin Cruise Lines, based in Miami and within one month one of his ex-partners filed a lawsuit to block it. Perhaps the luxury ship will make it to the Virgin Islands.

Don't worry; you won't have to worry about booking one of the Virgin ships. It is far more likely that a new arrival to cruise vacations will test the waters in a very medium price range.

It's easy to do. Go online and shop ships. See what ship fits your goals. After a few hours of pouring through the websites with excellent videos and snazzy offerings, you will undoubtedly have the ship-fitter blues. The choices are mind boggling.

Great ports abound in the Caribbean. Some are safer than others; all provide endless choices for beach days and tours. Cozumel, shown here, offers both. THE PRIVATEER CLAUSE photo

For the party-hardy crowd, there are plenty of opportunities to make your first cruise one you will never remember. The all-inclusive booze package on Carnival runs about fifty bucks a day, and the bar staff is supposed to cut you off after 15 drinks. If anyone can actually keep from falling off the rails while doing a re-creation of the Great Wallendas act, then that could have been a wise choice.

Carnival is a gaudy cruise line with a couple of high-drama disasters in recent years. The Costa Concordia capsized due to a real bozo of a captain.

That captain was recently convicted of manslaughter and should be hung from the gallows. Not likely to happen, but he deserves it.

Capt. Bozo claimed he fell into a lifeboat accidentally. Yeah. Right next to the First Officer and the Second Officer. The only thing that they didn't do was fall in alphabetically.

Then there was the engine room fire that disabled one of their ships off the coast of Mexico. Instead of being towed back to the closest port back in Mexico, Carnival management decided that somehow it was better for the ship to be at sea without power for four days while tugs would shove it across the Gulf of Mexico back to the U.S.

Apparently, any idiot can get a job as an executive at Carnival.

My adventure on the Carnival Miracle was all positive in that we didn't sink, and we didn't catch fire. If it didn't happen to you, it doesn't count!

The decor in the Carnival Miracle is incredible and adds to the voyage. THE PRIVATEER CLAUSE photo

It was a great ship, and the designer gave Gaudi a run for his money in the décor department. The food was excellent, and the entertainment was fun. Carnival proved that when they weren't torturing their customers, they could provide a great experience.

We didn't even have any drunken college kids take a dive from a balcony, at least none that anyone noticed. The sharks have to eat too.

Another Carnival-owned line that we have traveled on is Holland-America. As a guest speaker on ships, I have to say that this company knocks themselves out to accommodate speakers, as well as passengers. They have that Old Dutch salt feel to the design and fabric of the ships. One would never know there is any commonality with Carnival. The average age on Holland-America isn't quite pushing the Lawrence Welk crowd, but there are a few. Mostly the passengers weigh in (a joke) from about the fifties to eighties, with slight deviations below and above those age groups.

The Holland America ships are mostly what one would call small to medium size ships that accommodate about 1800 to 2000 passengers. They have officers that are Dutch, and décor and traditions are consistent with providing that legacy experience. The Holland America experience is quite good and just a shade above in price over the most competitive arena shared by NCL, Royal Caribbean, and Carnival.

With the Dutch flavor to Holland-America, one has to wonder why one of the cruise lines doesn't maintain a Vikings flavor with the staff dressed up in the cast of the History Channel series. I'll bet no one would let their kids pee in the pool, or the chair hogs would spread their towels around the best seats if the staff approached wearing horned helmets and carrying bloody swords.

The experience on Celebrity, which is owned by Royal Caribbean, is a bit upper-crusty. Think of a country club with all the men showing up at pre-dinner cocktail parties looking like they were auditioning for an ad in GQ and the women literally glowing in their new dresses and bling. The passengers even behave better on Holland and Celebrity. I'd bet they would all show proper deportment if the Vikings took over Carnival. But the passengers are another dimension to this CRUISE FACTS guide to picking out a cruise. We have plenty of time to discuss them later.

Celebrity lives up to their name in about every way possible. While taking a cruise on Carnival is like going on vacation with everyone you just met at the mall, Celebrity is almost like a trip with all those voted most likely to have good manners in high school.

I don't remember that being one of the categories in the silly contest that some oaf makes sure that graduating classes tally up in their high school yearbook, but if it were real, it would be a good way to describe Celebrity's passengers.

If your taste runs more to tattoos, boisterous behavior, and a thong show which shows things you wish you never saw, then NCL, Royal Caribbean's lower priced cruises, and Carnival would be your ticket.

CRUISE FACTS

The Holland-America Amsterdam travels through the Panama Canal
- THE PRIVATEER CLAUSE photo

Nick & Nora's Supper Club on the Carnival Miracle is one of the ship's pay to eat venues and offers a five-star experience.
THE PRIVATEER CLAUSE photo

CHAPTER TWO

The Food

Eating is an important part of taking a cruise, from the time one steps on board until the last moments before disembarking.

Not all food was created equal any more than the passengers who board ships to go down to the sea.

Having said that, which cruise line has the best food?

Ask anyone who has sailed on a ship and they are sure to have an opinion. While some may complain about the food from time to time and line to line, I can't recall having seen the Coast Guard have to evacuate anyone from a ship as a result of severe cases of failing to eat.

Brunch on a sea day on the Celebrity Equinox - THE PRIVATEER CLAUSE photo

The food is bountiful on all ships and can vary from mediocre to great on the same vessel.

An example of the first eating experience upon boarding a ship is the rush to the buffet while waiting for staterooms to be made available. While most folks are standing in line for as much as an hour or two if they get to the port early in the day; arriving just about two hours after the announced time for boarding will find swift entry to the ship, the ability to gain access to your stateroom and be able to unload all the junk you carried on.

CRUISE FACTS

The next bonus is the mad-house in the buffet area will likely be settling down. Additional food (yes they really do replenish the steam tables) will be brought out and probably untouched by your fellow passenger's sticky fingers and be hot.

Other eating venues such as the cafés and burger grills near pools are likely not to be as swamped and serve up the kind of quick fare you probably prepare at home. This is just the first couple of hours on board.

Most of the lines, from the big mega-ships down to the small vessels which have been renovated, now all have specialty restaurants. These small and mostly well-designed dining areas enjoy themes of Asian, Italian and beef house decors and menus. There are cover charges ranging from $20 up and offer a great place to get away from the smell of the crowd and the roar of the greasepaint in the buffet or the sometimes longer waits in the main dining room.

The menus tend to be more involved with more courses and feature appetizers and entrees worthy of upscale restaurants anywhere on land.

Watch the menu carefully as even though you are being charged an extra fee to eat in these specialty restaurants, some of them have additional fees for particular menu items of the more exclusive and expensive variety. These charges are not excessive, but they definitely will increase the cost of the meal more than you may have intended when you were seated.

Of course, keeping alert when ordering pays off when selecting a bottle of wine, whether in the main dining room or a specialty restaurant.

Many bottles of wine in the less than thirty dollar range can be excellent and if one has trouble polishing off a full bottle of wine at dinner, the waiter or sommelier will mark your room number on your bottle and have it available for you at your regular table in the main dining room or at any venue in which you choose to dine the next day.

Now that most cruise lines allow passengers to bring up to two bottles of wine on board when first boarding (not each port call) one should check the website of your cruise line for details. Some of the more luxury lines don't depend on blocking the boozers and wine lovers from bringing wine on board on port visits while others treat such items as contraband and snatch it from you to be returned on the last night of the cruise.

KEN ROSSIGNOL

A few specifics on specialty dining venues:

On Royal Caribbean, this medium price line is outfitting all their ships with upscale dining experiences and the ones we have tried did a remarkable job in selecting staff and menu options to meet the expectations.

On Holland America, the décor and amenities were polished and the food delicious.

Celebrity did a wonderful preparation of the dinners were ordered in several different ships, living up to their name in every way. From one of their oldest, the Mercury which has now been transferred and is sailing as Mein Schiff II to the new Solstice class Equinox and Eclipse; the upscale dining is well worth the extra money.

One of the best upscale dining experiences we enjoyed was on the Carnival Miracle in their Nick & Nora Supper Club. The decor and arrangements in the dining room were attractive and unique. The delivery on every aspect of the meal showed that Carnival was as adept as any cruise line or land-based restaurant to bring off an excellent meal. We enjoyed this restaurant's food and service immensely.

One can find an excellent meal at the regular dining times in the main dining rooms of all these lines, and there is no need to splurge unless it just sounds like fun.

Royal Caribbean has consistently good food, well-prepared and served by attentive staff. On dozens of trips, we have been waited on by less-than-stellar servers on only a couple of occasions. I am sure they were injected into the dining room directly to make the rest of the staff stand out.

This assessment of Royal Caribbean can also be made of the other lines and many ships on which we have traveled.

One of the best times to be on a ship might be immediately afterward or at the tail end of a Norovirus outbreak. This is when all the staff serves the passengers everything at the buffet while wearing plastic gloves.

What this means is that the disgusting habits of some of your fellow passengers don't get a chance to infect serving tongs and spoons with their germs to pass on to you. At tableside, the waiters dispense all condiments, salt and pepper and sweeteners for you without other passengers passing these containers to you.

Most of the lines have sanitizer stations at the entrances to each dining area, but it is amazing to see so many fail to avail themselves of the opportunity to become slightly less of a walking carrier of the highly contagious virus. (another chapter will review Norovirus)

On several Royal Caribbean ships, the pool-side Park Café is a hit. From panini sandwiches to fresh hot roast beef and soups; this venue provides quick service. A small salad bar which features a staffer assembling custom ordered salads to a small selection of hot steam-table food makes this tucked away café a great way to avoid the crowds in the Windjammer.

The main dining room experience at lunch is excellent with their large salad table with most every possible addition added to the order, once again with only staff handling utensils, and tossing your salad to perfection. Even with this, one can order a la carte from the menu.

The Windjammer continues to meet expectations for all meals and is an excellent alternative for dinner to the longer commitment of time in the main dining room.

Breakfast in the main dining room is usually superb. Entering port at San Juan on a ship while seated at a white-tablecloth-covered-table and being served Eggs Benedict as the shore glides by your large window is something many will never forget. How good does the food have to be in this setting?

Two chefs on Royal Caribbean ships, Grandeur and Serenade, docked in St. Maarten compares recipes. THE PRIVATEER CLAUSE photo

Being on the top deck is also neat, but there are plenty of chances to get that view; somehow it's just better when someone is serving you breakfast in a formal setting.

A great benefit to start the day is room service. If you are up earlier than when room service begins, usually about 6 am, there are large cauldrons of coffee set up near the pool decks of most ships or on the larger ships in the grand Park Central or equivalent.

Getting breakfast brought to your room is okay but opting for a fruit plate and large pot of coffee to wake up with as you get ready for a long day of adventure is the way to go. Most of the lines have a daily room service menu that passengers fill out the night before and select a delivery time. The choice list is then put out on the door handle before retiring.

The overall quality of the food varies from ship to ship and line to line. An assessment of the food on all the ships will vary from one person to another. I have to say all of them do a standout performance and are consistently good. The results of a poll of my readers on which cruise line has the best food will be posted on www.theprivateerclause.com website for your benefit.

Are some individuals not pleased with their meals?

Sure and most of them should be keel-hauled as they are hard to please in any setting and likely are miserable to live with at home. A review of passenger behavior will be coming up.

Every cruise line knocks themselves out to cater to those with food allergies or special dietary needs. Some advance notice at booking or boarding will find the staff to be accommodating.

An Aida ship leaves Cadiz, Spain. THE PRIVATEER CLAUSE photo

Chapter Three

Is Cruise Travel Safe?

Many cruises ago and many years ago as I sat near a pool on the deck of a ship I wondered how much trouble I could get into by writing about what I was observing. After giving some thought to how critical or appreciative analysis of bathing beauties and beached behemoths might not go over so well, my thoughts turned more to the 'what if' type of topic.

In the early nineties, as I helped my drivers get that week's edition of my weekly newspaper on the streets, I was listening to NPR only because the three am re-broadcast of the previous day's Rush Limbaugh show had finished. Not a real fan of the upper-crust and lefty-leaning of many NPR shows, my interest was peaked due to the author being interviewed, none other than one of my favorite writers, Stephen King.

King told of how he had gone nowhere in his attempts to write the Great American Novel. Finally, he decided to try his hand at writing thrillers and in doing so, found great success. King said that he learned that people just want the bejeebers scared out them.

They want ghost stories!

King has done an admirable job in his endeavor with many of his books becoming hit movies as well. I think of one of his books every time I cut the grass over the bones of my favorite pets planted near the edge of our garden.

I can attest to King's theory though I have yet to enjoy the success he has seen – thus far. One part of his philosophy that I have observed in my efforts to meet readers at book signings and speaking gigs is that people do indeed want to be told ghost stories and be titillated with fearful tales.

Whenever I am on a ship, regardless of the ocean, and the topic is the Bermuda Triangle, I have standing room only audiences packing the venue to hear me recite the tales of disappearing ships and planes in that mysterious section of the ocean.

I have to admit that there being so many occurrences of ocean vortexes and sudden clouds swallowing up boats and planes that while doing research or investigating such mysteries, which a chill can run down my spine.

That day that I considered King's words I decided to write the series known as the Marsha and Danny Jones Thrillers.

The entire premise is how the couple works to make cruise travel safe for the passengers of the Sea Empress. They have had some rough times in the process with the latest book "BEHEADED Terror By Land, Sea & Air" bringing ISIS to the table of death and destruction in the Caribbean.

While I work to bring realism to my books in this series I have also released FIRE CRUISE, which goes into great detail about crime, drugs, and fires on ships.

In this chapter, I want to discuss a broader look at cruise ship safety, especially for those who have never been on a cruise.

In a nutshell, I can assure you that cruise travel is the safest travel on earth except when it isn't.

For those who wonder why I am ducking into the Bermuda Triangle, bringing up stories of twenty-five-year-old radio interviews and dodging the topic – let me get to the bullet points.

- Is it safe to get drunk and play the Great Wallendas on the rail of a cruise ship?
- Will a rogue wave knock my ship over?
- Will pirates attack my ship and hold my mother-in-law hostage and demand a ransom?

CRUISE FACTS

The Celebrity Equinox in port at Tenerife, Canary Islands. THE PRIVATEER CLAUSE photo

As for the first question, go google "drunk college kids jump from cruise ship" and you'll see several instances of idiots doing just that with one guy proclaiming he was going to force the ship to turn around. For the record, it is impossible to fall over a railing on a ship. Those who go over are either tossed over as a result of homicidal intent or jump in the pursuit of suicide. The news pages will reveal some who jumped and swam or floated long enough to be found. Others have never been found due to the efficiency of the food chain practiced by the sea creatures.

In the instance of big waves, play around on Youtube to get your answer. There is no avoiding the videos of large waves rocking and rolling a ship. However, those instances occurred when the Captain of the ship failed to turn away from bad weather. Either those captains were ignorant or arrogant. It's easy to blame a corporate executive who may have wanted the ship to arrive in a port on time to keep the passengers on schedule with their tours. It just doesn't make sense to say that greed forced a Captain to endanger his ship and passengers and crew by sailing into the dangerous weather.

I have been on several ships where ports were skipped, and the course deviated to miss the rough weather. The damage that has occurred to ships which sailed into rough waters can easily soar into the millions and force a ship out of service for repairs. Being hit by high waves is a rare event and not likely to happen to you.

Now, the third scenario is a tough one. First, there are events in recent years where pirates have attacked ships off the coast of Somalia. None has been successful and future attacks are not likely as multi-national warships aggressively patrol those areas. Given the rise of ISIS in the world, anything is possible. For now, your mother-in-law is safe. She may never find out you refused to go her ransom and offered to pay the pirates to keep her.

The continuing use of passengers and crew to work as mules for drug trafficking remains a danger to everyone on a ship. The use of drugs by passengers and crew has risks for others.

The sloppy way that cruise lines hire and fail to adequately screen for criminals presents a risk. This is one area that could use improvement. The small number of arrests of the crew for assaults on passengers is dwarfed by the total number of the crew working on ships.

One recent exception was the sexual attack on a passenger by a crewman who restocked the mini bars on the Quantum of The Seas, one of Royal Caribbean's newest hi-tech ships. Unfortunately, the technology being touted in their advertising didn't also include a way for that assailant to have his key card deactivated when he was off-duty. He entered a woman's stateroom and attacked her during the night. That man was recently convicted and sentenced to a federal prison so he won't have a chance to rack up another assault anytime soon.

Many ports are dangerous and exceedingly so in much of the Caribbean. These islands host criminal elements that view tourists as easy marks and frustrate the efforts of their governments to attract and keep visits by cruise ships to their ports. Bandits have robbed an entire busload of cruise passengers at St. Kitts, tourists have been murdered at St. Lucia and St. Maarten and San Juan and St. Thomas have homicide rates equal to or higher than mainland American cities.

The cruise lines could and should empathize safety and avoidance of lone ventures into cities, towns or off-the-beaten-track beach areas. The island criminals are only waiting to strike and sometimes walk in packs along the beaches looking for the goodies lying in the sand next to unguarded towels and chairs.

The bottom line is that your safety is your responsibility.

Stick to the areas where you see the police officers in St. Kitts. They are there to protect the tourists. Wandering off on side streets shows the criminals that you are not only a bit daffy but an easy mark.
THE PRIVATEER CLAUSE photo

Capt. Kenny Sunshine will knock himself out to give a great tour of St. Kitts, including stops to see his Uncle's monkey, his mom, and this great view of both the Atlantic and the Caribbean from a roadside pull off. THE PRIVATEER CLAUSE photo

CHAPTER FOUR

Danger lurks on every cruise...

That phrase is a subtitle for my Marsha & Danny Jones Thrillers, and while those books are fiction, the hype line sure applies in the real world of cruising as well. Now, many of you might think, big deal, life is full of dangers, just try walking through a parking lot to the entrance of Walmart.

The difference between driving on a typical American freeway, entering a store with a Black Friday sale or riding a subway, is that in those situations, there is an expectancy of peril. When you book a cruise, there is a likelihood of safety.

There is no reason you should not expect to disembark from your cruise vacation intact, perhaps heftier on the scales due to all that food and lighter in the wallet due to all the new ship fees. That is the average person – there are always aberrations, which is the reason we have "news". The unusual, the exceptional and the tragic all make the news on land, and the same is true at sea.

There have been seven recent drownings or near drownings of children which have taken place on all the major cruise lines due to two reasons.

First, parents who have an expectancy of safety on this cruise that is costing the family plenty; and second, the lawyers for the cruise lines believe that posting signs next to pools noting there is no lifeguard on duty is all the precaution that their cruise line must exercise.

Well, we know how well those "don't tiptoe on the railings" signs are working out and the same goes for the signs next to the pools.

To make matters worse when a pool tragedy gets underway, the staff usually goes into this typical scenario, according to witness reports.

First, the staff that is nearby to a drowning is usually not the same staff that just MAYBE had some sort of lifesaving training. That nearby crew member is likely the guy hawking the tray full of drinks and has a slight command of English and none of CPR.

Second, the security staff who rush to the scene also suffer from a lack of actually having equipment other than a radio and a badge. The lifesaving equipment that is on the ship is usually not near the pool but many decks below, maybe ten or so, in the medical center. That means that someone has to fetch the medical equipment and bring it back to the confused panic-stricken crew members. But the security guys are good at giving passengers orders.

In a recent drowning on the NCL Gem, the witnesses reported that a qualified nurse passenger was ordered to stand away from the child and not render aid or be "arrested".

In twenty-five years of being a police beat reporter responding to life-threatening news events, not once did I ever see a real police officer order anyone attempting to aid an accident victim prior to the arrival of rescue units to stand back or be arrested. Part of that reason is that the cops themselves had first aid training and were rendering assistance instead of worrying about crowd control.

This situation on NCL would be reason enough for me to never board one of their ships but since all the cruise lines except Disney still refuse to provide lifeguards, more tragedy can be expected of the Gem type of scenario at any time.

Would parents actually be watching their children instead of letting them have free run of the ship, of course, there would be fewer drownings.

Passengers on ships need to remember that the 41 page contract that you sign covers every type of cruise line negligence and that the contract is written to protect the cruise company, not to ensure your satisfaction and safety. That you are satisfied and kept safe is entirely incidental.

The odds are on the side that you will have a safe trip, not be mugged on or off the ship and arrive home without contracting Norovirus.

It is only when tragedy does strike that "normal" goes out the window.

In my book Fire Cruise, I present many factual cases of crime on ships and in popular Caribbean ports and thus rather than duplicate that information here, will instead continue on describing unsafe practices and how to keep from being a statistic.

Other than drownings and falling from railings while showing off to drunken friends, what are other dangers?

Lots of cruises cater to older crowds. The experience of being on a ship is actually so positive for the geezer crowd that many can boast of being on fifty or more cruises. Some spend much of a year on a vessel and point out that the cost is cheaper than an assisted living center or nursing home – and one is treated nicer on a ship.

All true.

What is risky is for older guests to take a fall when a ship hits rough weather.

The hallways in ships have railings as do all stairs and elevators. The downside is actually touching the railings with your hands quickly advances the odds of getting Norovirus.

When the ship starts rocking is the time for older guests to hunker down in their rooms or move cautiously. Some move to using wheelchairs as a guard against a tumble.

For the folks who travel and put all their faith in God and their St. Christopher medal, I say keep up the good work. One needs all the faith and prayers possible to keep you safe.

That wonderful crew member who stocks the minibar in your room has a key. A master key. What the cruise lines don't do is monitor the use of that key card or restrict it when the employee is not working. Now, one would think that would be an easy task to accomplish in the interest of passenger safety.

The world's newest and most technology-advanced ship, the Quantum of The Seas rolled out last year for Royal Caribbean. Unfortunately, that ship had a crewmember who flew into a rage when a passenger told him "get lost you" and called him an SOB when he attempted to enter her stateroom to service the minibar. He returned later that night when she was alone and asleep and raped and beat her and would have murdered her as well had she not fought back. He escaped out the balcony and hopped to another balcony as the victim ran out of the room into a hallway seeking help. He was convicted recently and will serve time in federal prison.

Since I am on the mailing list for the FBI, I read the report from the U.S. Attorney of the conviction. The press release by the FBI didn't mention the name of the ship or the cruise line. The media is not shy about jumping on Carnival over torturing their customers in the Gulf or the latest ship with Norovirus. But virtually none of the media carried the name of the vessel or cruise line when they published the press release from the feds. Why? The media, by and large, at least the ones who still have jobs – are lazy. Much of the media depends on the law enforcement agencies to spoon feed them and you, as a consumer, are the recipient of the end product of pablum. With only about five minutes work, I was able to find the original arrest reports of the criminal crewman's ship and cruise line and included both in my news report.

I think it's very significant that Royal Caribbean is boasting of swiveling you at 360 degrees in the air from the top of the ship, out over the sea, in a thrill ride, while they can't monitor and limit the use of a master key for passenger staterooms at the time the employee is not working, and the passenger is in bed.

Exactly how safe do you think that little thrill ride in the glass bubble is going to be on the newest class of Royal ships?

For one, I am glad they are sending these ships to work the China ports.

The cruise lines are pretty strict about the conduct of the crew. Most of the crew I have had contact with on ships are hard-working, polite and professional in delivering a great experience to passengers. I have traveled so many thousands of miles on vessels and found so many wonderful people working on ships that it is my expectation that most readers will too.

Again, the very definition of "news" is when events and situations are out of the ordinary. Don't confuse those big portions of oatmeal dressed up as network morning news shows as actual news. They aren't. Those shows are designed only for ratings and revenue from advertisers. Period.

If it weren't for disasters to be able to stretch out those morning shows or fill every hour for cable news, the airwaves would be filled with Kardashians.

What other perils are available to spoil your cruise.

Given that this chapter, and much of the book, won't get into the crime on shore – and if you don't plan on it being there to greet your visit you are simply a "denier", and I won't bother to ask you who you voted for in the recent elections.

I covered the speaking needs of a beautiful ship from Bayonne for a couple of months, as I was booked for three cruises and then asked to fill in for another speaker who had become ill for three more. The ship is one of Royal Caribbean's largest and has been recently refurbished in 2015. The Explorer of The Seas is quite a production choreographed by an excellent staff of crew, hotel workers, restaurant personnel and entertainment staff. All of the ships must present a never-ending cycle of service to passengers year in and year out.

They work really hard to achieve their goals and sometimes they fail to do so. It takes a real ironic set of circumstances for failure to set in, but I'll leave the nitpicking to the bitter and nasty passengers who dump on the cruise lines on Cruise Critic reviews. Many Cruise Critic members do their best to set the record straight about false and flame-war reviews castigating a ship's staff unfairly. Most readers can spot those cases and make up their own minds.

To get the point. When I was on the Explorer for two months straight, one of the trips was a short one, just five days. The cruise director noted that I hadn't seen one of the short voyages before to Bermuda from New York and he said, "it's a different type of crowd" and laughed as he went on to tend to the boarding of the next set of passengers.

Later that night I realized what he meant as the party-hardy crowd was returning to their cabin next to me after the bars closed for the night. In a nutshell, that cruise was cheap and a popular rock band from the New York and New Jersey area was onboard with about five hundred of their fans. It was a zoo. Cheap has its price to pay for the unsuspecting.

Being able to pick who you are traveling with is problematic. Some folks have arrived on their trip to find out that the majority of passengers were of a different persuasion than themselves. To surmise that traditional church folks from Ohio might not like being on a Celebrity voyage with about 1500 gays would be an understatement. The church folks would have a lot to talk about when they got back to Peoria.

There can be significant advantages as well.

On one Celebrity voyage, the Baltimore Symphony Orchestra was on board our ship for the eleven-day trip to the Caribbean. Towards the end of the journey, the long-hairs must have been in a good mood and invited all passengers to attend a free concert. Otherwise, their performances had been only available to those who paid a premium fare to join their special cruise. The orchestra for the ship, any ship, is always great, but a symphony at sea can be spectacular. I didn't attend, my wife did and loved it. I went instead to listen to my friend Bruce Caplan give a lecture on the Titanic.

There is a way to find out if any large groups are on your cruise. There are two ways. First, ask your travel agent or cruise line reservation clerk. They should have a special notation on their computers about big groups. Second, go to Cruise Critic and nose around the Boards for postings for your anticipated cruise as lots of passengers scour the internet looking for incidentals to exchange as the anticipation for their looming cruise grows. That is an excellent way to find lower cost shore excursions looking for a few more people to fill their van. That is a great way to save but off-topic for this chapter.

Thus, now you have an idea about how to avoid the annual convention of the Leper Pickpocket Society of Detroit's Cruise.

Surfrider on the Independence of the Seas.
The Privateer Clause photos

The Captain of the Explorer of the Seas at work on the bridge. The Captain uses a chart to get where he is going and, like any man – never, never stops to ask a clerk in a 7-Eleven for directions.
. THE PRIVATEER CLAUSE photo

Chapter Five

How to visit San Juan without getting mugged

SAN JUAN, P. R. --- The ability of the visitor to find a visit to San Juan to be positive depends on how much awareness one wants to show. This is a beautiful Caribbean island, steeped in history, blessed with wonderful weather and people with many wonderful folks all wishing to greet you to their land. Then there are the criminals.

Puerto Rico has a higher crime rate than New York City. A lot higher. Nine times higher, according to Trip Advisor.

When a visitor arrives in San Juan on a cruise ship, the entrance to the harbor is setting unique to its location and dripping in history. On the port side of your ship as it enters is the old Fort that guarded the harbor against whatever nation wished to conquer the island – usually the English wishing to boot out the Spanish. The bleached walls that reach high above the rocky shore are impenetrable. Access to the Old San Juan is through massive gates on the harbor side and high walls surround the old city.

When a ship arrives at the large cruise terminal, the passengers move down the long dock towards a waiting line of taxis, vans, and buses ready to pick up their tour groups or book private tours. The drivers seeking their fares for the day are eager to please, and the wise visitor should book one of these drivers instead of free-lancing a day in the port.

The immediate three or four blocks directly above the terminal are safe for shopping the store's open-air markets. Many of the cafes also have outdoor seating and free Wi-Fi is available everywhere for those skipped booking the high-priced internet on the ship. This is the time to catch up on emails back home. Since this is a United States territory, those who are U. S. residents can make phone calls as soon as they were within about a mile of the island and talk at the same rate as their respective plans allow them on the mainland.

In most cases, your ship will arrive in the morning or early afternoon. Stick to Old San Juan and the area immediately adjacent to the ship if walking. Night-time is dangerous anywhere outside of this area. A day is walking and shopping while sightseeing along the plaza near the harbor, passing through the Gates of San Juan and into the Old San Juan is a once in a lifetime experience.

San Juan is one of the few, and perhaps the only American city bombarded by the U. S. Navy – if you don't count the Civil War.

The stroll along the edge of the harbor with the tall walls on your right allows one to imagine being on the outside of the walls as the American Navy blasted the Spanish during the Spanish-American War.

The Cathedral contains the remains of Ponce De Leon and is carefully maintained and historic place of worship.

The shops, restaurants and art galleries can easily fill a day's time. As the day grows longer, one will notice the many police officers visible and on patrol. They do a good job and are severely needed.

With almost four million people living on the island, Puerto Rico had 681 homicides in 2014 while Baltimore, Md. with about 650,000 population has had 250 murders in ten months of 2015.

KEN ROSSIGNOL

While Baltimore's crime rate soars, the crime rate in Puerto Rico has been declining. There were 1,164 murders in Puerto Rico in 2011.

Compounding the crime on the part of criminals in Puerto Rico was a crime on the part of the police. So much public corruption was revealed that the FBI stepped into handle serious felonies and were responsible for much of the drop in the crime rate as conviction rates soared. Criminals went to federal prisons and life got a lot better for both residents and tourists.

Many of other Puerto Rican cities are in serious decline with high unemployment, street crime, violent car-jackings and gang warfare. The Commonwealth is over $70 Billion in debt, and young people are fleeing the island for a better life in Florida and other states.

A bustling San Juan belies the welfare state massive debt that looms over the island in addition to crime. THE PRVIATEER CLAUSE photo

There are few places that offer more of a glimpse into history than Old San Juan. This guard tower looked out on the ocean to give warning of an impending attack by a foreign fleet of warships.
THE PRIVATEER CLAUSE photo

Chapter Six

How to book a Cheapo Cruise!

Veteran cruisers can skip this chapter. You already know strategies for enjoying a nice cruise for the lowest amount out of pocket. You have already gained return customer status in the various cruise line programs for repeat customers. Congratulations!

I had been on ships when the cruise director announced the names of passengers who had been on their 50th, 75th and even 100th cruise. By the time that they get to that status, many have built up credits for free cruises, and their voyage may be just to meet old friends among passengers, officers, and crew. Upgrades include just about anything the ship offers, up to and including a suite, champagne and perhaps a massage.

However, if you are among those getting your feet wet, well, not literally, the whole idea is to remain above the waterline, then this chapter is for you.

Building a relationship with a travel agent is important. In the beginning, it's helpful to have a knowledgeable person guide you to what works and away from what might not work for you.

We have worked with a great representative of one large agency, and she did an excellent job.

You may believe that since you have a computer and access to all sorts of travel agencies and direct access to the cruise line's websites that you don't need an agent.

Chances are, you may be one hundred percent right. Sail on, veterans and newbies! You are well-equipped to navigate the choppy waters of cruise line pricing.

Now for folks who believe that are plenty of ways to learn new techniques, I'll try to share some with you.

First, become familiar with online resources. Sure, you can sign up for all those glossy brochures that the cruise lines still send out, and some are expensive productions designed to peak your interest and make you reach out and touch them with your credit card.

The best resource is Cruise Critic. While they are owned by a travel agency and occasionally let their corporate life get in the way of their objectivity, it's rare for that to happen.

When big waves crash into ships that should have avoided storms, I have seen them carry pretty good news stories of the events. Same goes for when cruise passengers were murdered in Tunisia. What idiot executive thought that port visit was a good idea is beyond me.

Why is it that corporate executives of the cruise lines always come up with strategies to avoid disasters after the fact?

Well, back to Cruise Critic.

The website's editors take lots of free cruises where the cruise lines know exactly who they are, never charge them for a thing and lavish great treatment on them. While Cruise Critic editors are far from objective, they do provide a fair assessment of the ships they travel.

The best review is always the member review.

When driving for a few hours with my wife – she always drives as she is a control freak, as well as a good driver and I like having a chauffeur – I often read the member reviews of ships we have traveled on to pass the time. I read them aloud. It's always good for more than a few laughs.

I am encouraging you to read them too but suspend your disbelief. Some of these review writers are nasty and arrogant people and don't mind letting the world see that as long as they hide behind a screen name. What could be worse is that you might be stuck with these miserable souls on the same ship for a week or two. Count your blessings.

Many of these negative reviews of ships are unfair and deceitful.

Most of them are spot on, and the discerning reader should be able to tell the difference and laugh at the idiots bent on vengeance for a slow flushing toilet and take a few pointers from those who make honest and blunt reports.

The best thing to learn about pricing and deals from some of the members of Cruise Critic is not from the reviews. Go to the Boards of Cruise Critic. Select the ship on which you plan to sail and hidden among the many routine postings such as 'we need to meet when we board and all wear something to recognize each other.' Those folks have already made friends on the Boards and will perpetrate those liaisons to the cruise. Some will host a pre-cruise brunch with lots of good food for others booked for the cruise who live within one hundred miles of each other.

We've been to them, and it's a great way to meet some nice folks and to spend a Sunday afternoon.

The real value from meeting on the boards or a pre-cruise party is to gain those gems of how to get a great fare or the much sought-after "upgrade".

Here is a real-life example.

We wanted to take a cruise on a Celebrity ship based in Baltimore. The line doesn't have one there now; they sold the Mercury to subsidiary, Tui Lines and it had about $55 million spent on it four years ago. It now travels the high seas as the Mein Schiff II.

We decided about eight months in advance to book an eleven-night trip to the Caribbean with stops at St. Maarten, St. Kitts, St. Thomas, St. John Antiqua and St. Croix. Our balcony stateroom was supposed to run about $1600 double occupancy.

We booked this through the large internet travel agency Cruises Only (there are quite a few). This is when the internet searches on an almost daily basis come in handy. Keep checking the sailing specials for your booking each and every day. It only takes a minute.

One day you will click to your sailing page for your ship and Bingo! There will be a special sale on the same accommodations you are booked for at full price. This is where your excellent relationship with your friendly travel agent comes to play. Call him or her and ask them very nicely if they could get you an upgrade. While some lines offer price protection, many don't any longer. The best you can hope for is an upgrade and from what you will learn on the Boards at Cruise Critic, they are rare.

On this particular cruise, we did get a better cabin – a suite complete with our own maid and butler. Sure, we had to share them with about a dozen other suites, but still, we liked them. The suite came with a full-size tub, a balcony that was oversized and could fit about a dozen lounge chairs and plates of good grub in the afternoon.

My point: we got this upgrade due to using the same agent (Barbara Nason) for several cruises and for sending friends to her as well. We would have enjoyed the cruise just as much with an inside cabin, as we have had dozens of those staterooms. But balconies and suites are nice too.

This same agent also recommended the right hotel for us; that was affiliated with Celebrity in Rome. It worked nicely for us to be lodged there as the entire city was within walking distance or a brief walk to the bus stop for the hop on, hop off.

So follow this tip trail.

Learn tips on bookings and snatching great deals from your fellow cruisers on the Boards at Cruise Critic. Most of the folks there are very different from the bozos who leave nasty reviews on the ship. These are vivacious veterans or enthusiastic newbies off to enjoy the greatest adventure of their lives.

There are far more great tips here than simply how to book a cheap cruise.

Some point out the wisdom of booking a hotel for $99 which allows you to park your car for free for the duration of your cruise and shuttles you free of charge to the port. That's a deal.

One time I was looking for bus transportation from Washington, D.C. to Bayonne, New Jersey at Cape Liberty. Sure, Google might have revealed that information, but in the Boards, I picked up detailed info. I had to meet a ship for three back to back cruises on which I was the speaker on maritime history, the Titanic, piracy and the Bermuda Triangle and this time I was going alone as my wife was staying home for our grandson's First Communion. We had already been on the same ship, the fantastic Explorer of the Seas twice that spring and would be back on it in six weeks – after I returned from spending a month at sea.

Thus, I was going to be without my driver and who wants to pay to park for a month in New Jersey?

The bus was great.

Academy runs pickups in Washington, Baltimore, Wilmington, Philadelphia and then on to Port Liberty. They run similar buses from all around the region. Check their website.

They provide cruise transfers for Royal Caribbean, NCL, and Celebrity.

Academy's rate of $100 per person roundtrip from pickup locations in the mid-Atlantic region, including Virginia, Maryland, Connecticut, Pennsylvania, Rhode Island, New Jersey and Massachusetts was in effect in October of 2015 for sailings on the new Royal Caribbean Anthem of The Seas at Cape Liberty.

The buses are as advertised: clean, free WIFI, courteous and friendly drivers, have electrical outlets to plug in your electronics and large flat screen TV. The time passes quickly.

The pickup spot near Baltimore is an easy one, as the motel will allow you to leave your vehicle there if you spent the night there.

This is usually the same deal with most hotels anywhere in the nation near a port. Check them out when booking your room and get written confirmation in advance or don't book your accommodations there. This isn't necessary if you are flying to the port, but the FREE shuttle from the hotel to the port is a benefit you will enjoy.

Academy and other bus lines feature online booking, and you print out your tickets, much like anything else. Always save the ticket in your smartphone too in case you lose your paper tickets.

One of the tips you will soon discover in Cruise Critic Boards is the advice from your fellow world travelers that last minute deals are great.

That's true. No cruise ship leaves port with empty rooms. At least not on purpose.

Some folks cancel at the last minute. Some kick the bucket. A few might land in prison. Whatever the reason, there may be vacant cabins after boarding, and a tip to the hotel director might get you an upgrade.

But, how can you land a cheapo deal?

Think obstructed view cabins. Every ship has them. There are not any obstructed views in inside staterooms. Those with views are always on the outside of the ship unless you are on one of the goliaths with the big central parks.

Last minute bookings are where you get the deals. Cruise lines are going to fill every room. Travel agencies that buy big blocks of staterooms are going to release them but they truly want to fill them. This is where your dexterity and nimble fingers on the keyboard comes in handy. You can use an agent to steer you to a great deal or do it yourself.

You may learn one morning in the main dining room at a table for 12 that there are people at your table that paid $2500 each for a balcony stateroom while another couple with the same accommodations paid half that amount. The bookings were soft during the recession, at the same time the new ships which had been ordered before the recession began to float out of the shipyards in Europe.

Thus, the cruise lines had a contraction in the world economy at the same time there was an expansion in the number of staterooms available on dozens of new ships. The result, the nearly 20 million folks, taking a cruise in 2009 thru 2014 found great bargains. The mess Carnival made out of the industry with its disasters added to the fray of profits and losses.

Since the public has short memories and the Costa Concordia has finally been hauled away from view to be scrapped, folks are less worried about visiting Davy Jones's Locker.

Short Trips

Three and four-night cruises out of ports with lots of ships can bring advertised prices as low as "from $149" as Royal Caribbean features for a three night Bahamas Cruise. Great deal, yes. This cruise is on Royal's oldest and smallest ship. The cruise leaves from Miami and visits Nassau and Royal Caribbean's private island at CocoCay. My advice for those who have a port visit in the Bahamas is to simply stay on the ship. Crime is prime in that nation. At least the Prime Minister recently had a home invasion at his residence so he can see what's it like for the average person. Sure, you can book a tour to a beach, but who is riding shotgun, you might ask. No one. Stay on the ship. The Royal Caribbean private islands such as Coco Cay and Labadie are well-designed experiences which can provide a fun trip and great memories.

CRUISE FACTS

Royal Caribbean also takes care of its older ships with refurbishments in every possible venue and attribute. I like them and believe they offer excellent value.

I also like Holland America and believe Celebrity is tops. We have taken a nice trip on Carnival as well. Carnival is like going on a cruise with everyone you just saw at the mall. Celebrity is much like a country club setting with folks exercising good taste. Royal is everything in between.

You can use the same guide on a ship these days as you use in Walmart to learn more about the culture of your fellow passengers by noting the body piercings and counting the tattoos.

The cruise lines offer three and four-night trips from Rome and Southampton at low rates which are great for those already there and don't need to fly there from North America.

Many short trips from New York, New Jersey, and Florida are simply booze cruises. Carnival is selling all-inclusive booze packages. They claim they will cut off a liquor customer after 15 drinks in a day. How much fun can this be to be stuck with a couple of thousand lushes for three days? But you did get a cheap cruise.

Off-Season Rates

There really isn't an off-season for cruise lines. They move ships from one area of the world to another because they float and are easy to move. Alaska's season ends in the fall and ships are moved to Pacific ports, trans-canal trips to the Caribbean and back and forth for the winter before returning to Alaska. Ships in the Med in the spring, summer, and fall flock across the Atlantic to partake in the intense Caribbean trade in the winter.

One particular time to book and find some soft rates are the time period for about two to three weeks between Thanksgiving and just before Christmas. We have found great rates in the Caribbean as well as for about two to three weeks after the New Year in January. The last minute bookings will reveal the best deals. Keep your bags packed and be flexible. This is a good time to get out of northern climes anyway.

Trans-Atlantic

In the spring and the fall, there are many excellent bargains for those who enjoy sea days. We have taken a couple, and I loved it. It was like having two cruises in one. From Rome, after spending four days exploring the incredible art and architecture of the Vatican and Rome, we set off for the New World. First, we had a week in the Mediterranean, and the weather was mild if you don't count a full day of vigorous rain in Livorno. So we stayed on the ship. The Celebrity Equinox is well appointed and a great and fun ship. Plenty to do when it's raining cats and dogs who all speak Italian.

With port visits in Cannes, France; Seville via Cadiz; Cartagena and Barcelona, our bus tours to the Royal Palace and the fantastic Cathedral of the Holy Family, were great.

Arranging tours with Spain Day Tours and other outfits found in the Cruise Critic Boards made for great savings. The cruise lines always give you the hard sell for their tours by stressing that ship-sponsored tours always will find the Captain holding the ship at the dock for you. The inference is that your hotel will glide out of the harbor when your tardy tour which had a flat tire manages to lumber into the parking lot.

Not really true or likely. You always have a phone number for the ship to make a panicked call to wait and most of the time, the ship will. The real protection is for bad weather forcing the ship to miss a port. Then the cruise line will make it up to you either by having bus meet your ship at the replacement port and enable you to drive to the original destination, if that is possible, or give you a refund. It's hit or miss what the private tour folks will do with your paid in advance tour.

Lots of Boards folks will book a day tour in an eight passenger van, so your day in port is more flexible than being one of fifty to sixty on the large charter bus. Then on the Board postings, they will advertise that they have room for a few more people to fill the van. We have done this, and it worked fine. I felt sorry for one nice optometrist from Florida who booked us into his van for a trip from Cherbourg to the Normandy Beaches. One of the couples who were with us stiffed him when we got back to the ship, leaving him paying for them as well as his portion for him and his wife.

We've done plenty of the big tour buses, and I have to admit to not having any complaints. They tend to be roomier than the eight-passenger vans. Either one will give you the willies going around mountain curves like we had on the island of Madeira off of Portugal.

CRUISE FACTS

Oasis of the Seas near Cuba. THE PRIVATEER CLAUSE photo

Back to the bargain fare for a trans-Atlantic voyage.

The cruise lines will let a T/A go for as low as $500 per person for an inside cabin.

Royal offered an inside cabin on its new tech-savvy Anthem of The Seas from Southampton to Cape Liberty in New Jersey for only $749, a $200 savings from its previously set rate. The amazing Allure of The Seas had a rate of $798 for a T/A from Barcelona to Fort Lauderdale. The competition for the cruise lines in filling these ships to return to Europe is so fierce, that even now eighteen months in advance one can book passage on the beautiful Rhapsody of The Seas for a Sixteen-night voyage from Tampa, Florida to Rome in April of 2017 for just $807 per person.

Folks, this is more than two weeks of someone else making your bed, picking up the towels, bringing you hot coffee and buns while you get dressed in the morning, providing a half dozen or more places for you to dine and putting on fun shows and entertainment.

Invariably, some crank will write a review in Cruise Critic that they spied rust on a railing somewhere. Those muttonheads have no idea how corrosive the salt air is to metal and abusive to paint. Constant maintenance is needed, and often weather prevents that work from being done. That is why the thoughtful reader will take those reviews with a grain of "salt".

Most of the trans-Atlantic trips consist of eight sea days and usually stop in at Tenerife or the Azores on the way across. The new Anthem is taking the North Atlantic direct route to the Hudson River in November of 2016. The more typical trips of 13 to 16 days include the crossing and lots of neat port visits to Spain, France, Portugal and Italy. We have enjoyed them all, and the variety provides most folks with the ability to take day tours to Paris, London and Rome on their respective voyages – just not at the same time!

The highest price times to sail

Avoid booking a cruise at Christmas or peak summer season. Rates are higher then and remember – this is when children roam the seven seas.

There are two forms of travel – First Class – and with children.

The kids are cute if they are your children or grandchildren. Otherwise, they are just noisy rug-rats. Fall and spring are great times to find good fares and a lack of kids. Except for spring or Easter break. We have been on a ship on Easter break that left from Southampton with about 1500 English children on board for a round trip to the Canaries. Royal Caribbean had to post elevator operators in each elevator. Other than that the children were okay.

Watch for price drops on Cruise Critic

Cruise Critic, along with other travel websites, will post what they call "Price Drops." Some are for real while others are just hype. Become educated and you will reap the rewards.

For instance, on Oct. 22, 2015, Cruise Critic advertised a voyage for Dec. 21, 2015 on the Celebrity Constellation. The Constellation has undergone several refits from the time it was first launched and features most of the great appointments that the newest Celebrity ships have. An inside cabin on a five-night trip from Fort Lauderdale to the Western Caribbean had been advertised for $1,598 was listed as available for $409 for an inside cabin, per person. That is a bargain, as long as a caller can pick up the deal when clicking through on the buy button. This is a peak time and over Christmas, the ship is nicely decorated as are the port towns on the itinerary. Another bargain for the west coast travelers is a Crown Princess voyage on the Mexican Riviera for seven nights out of Los Angeles with a Suite, which had been advertised for $5,698 for just $989 per person. Princess enjoys an excellent reputation and anyone who booked a suite with a bargain price for the Nov. 14, 2015, cruise will understand that when I advise you that every ship leaves full, it's likely pretty much on the mark.

After all, if the ship leaves without you, how will they make money upselling you all the great meals, booze, and massages or see you in the casino. Better to fill up the remaining cabins at cheapo prices than make less once underway. Their staff is there to attend to the maximum passengers. Therefore, the cruise lines have the incentive to maximize their investment to reach their profit goals. That won't happen with empty cabins.

For one more example try this Trans-Atlantic deal on the Costa Magica leaving Genoa on Nov. 28, 2015. The price has been dropped from $999 to $399 per person for an inside cabin. This is a 15-night voyage. Costa is clearly making sure all cabins are full at this price. Those with miles to cash in may find the time periods blocked thus airfare to Italy is the key.

A trip to the web finds British Airways offering tickets for two seniors for $1130 each via Heathrow to Italy. Smartfares.com offers tickets for $596 on Turkish Airways connected through Istanbul, Turkey after leaving from Dulles IAD near Washington. This fare is for Nov. 23rd which allows a few days' tour Genoa and around Italy before leaving on your cheapo cruise back to the United States.

Now that you have found a cheap flight from America to Italy, even if you have to connect through Turkey, it's time to learn more about your cruise. Go back to Cruise Critic and click to learn which port in the U. S. the ship arrives. It doesn't and in fact, the price now has gone up to $668, evidently to you taking too much time finding a deal on the airfare. But still, that is only $200 more for you and your spouse. Where do you wind up?

This cruise is to the Caribbean and includes stops in nice ports. St. Maarten, St. John Antiqua, Fort De France in Martinique and Pointe a Petra on Guadeloupe. Now you either stay on the ship for another seven hundred bucks each and visit four more ports, pick up another sea day and end up again at Guadeloupe. Therefore, your cheap cruise from Italy includes an elegant Caribbean cruise as well, all for $1598 each, which, as far as cruise travel goes, is a great bargain.

But now you have to fly home to the U.S. or Canada.

A cruise on the Celebrity Silhouette on Oct. 31, 2015, was advertised as $699 each for an inside cabin and says the price dropped from $1,399. That statement on Cruise Critic sounds like a lot of hype as one could probably have booked that rate last spring instead of a week before the ship sails. At $699, this ship is a bargain and having done two trans-Atlantic crossings on the Celebrity Equinox and Eclipse; I can assure anyone that they will enjoy this ship as it is the first in the class and has been refurbished once already since being launched in 2008. This cruise leaves from Rome and arrives in Fort Lauderdale. But the date is different for airfare.

Now for this, change to a ship that actually makes it all the way to the United States, back to smartfares.com finds a choice of Aeroflot or Turkish Airlines for $597 each on Oct. 27th. The Russian plane might have free vodka, and their flight is one dollar cheaper. Jet Blue offers flights that connect in Dublin for $882 each.

Now your cheapo cruise is running $700 each for the ship and $600 each for the flight. Airport transfers, your hotel, sightseeing and fun in Rome is all out of pocket, but Celebrity offers great deals on booking through them for your hotel, which worked fine for us. They also offer a last minute tour on the day your ship leaves Rome and will pack you up along with your luggage, lug you out to the Coliseum and then haul you off to meet your ship. Pretty convenient.

This price is one heckuva lot lower than the one we booked by planning it six months in advance.

Should you book these arrangements, be sure to send me an email from the ship.

ken@theprivateerclause.com

By the way, this ship stops at Florence for great day trips; Toulon France; Barcelona; Palma De Mallorca, Spain; Tenerife in the Canary Islands and then on to Fort Lauderdale. This is a great itinerary, and when we traveled this same schedule, we found the weather to be warm, and there were plenty of sea days by the pool in this fall sailing. Celebrity does a great job. And don't miss the trip to the Cathedral in Barcelona.

Chapter Seven

Cruise ship raid nets $31 million in cocaine and three arrests in Sydney

Austrailian Police provided this photo of part of the $31 million in cocaine seized from a passenger's luggage when the ship arrived in port.

Three's Company in a pricey suite on a cruise ship but not in the slammer for Isabelle Legace, Andre Tamine, and Melina Roberge on the Sea Princess.

That was the bottom line for an adventurous pair of good-looking gals who hooked up with an old guy who evidently paid for a $20,000 cruise to some of the world's most glamorous exotic islands and ports.

While a young woman may have carried a diary in her luggage fifty years ago, today's modern traveler often keeps their diary in the 'cloud' and sends posts of her adventure on social media sites like Instagram, keeping her friends and family up to date on daily happenings.

Roberge posted this to her Instagram account:

KEN ROSSIGNOL

Melinar___First time in Papeete and not the last one ✌😎

The comments on Facebook Page of the police ranged from congratulations to the law enforcement agencies to support for the coke-smuggling accused who may be spending their future tan time in a prison yard.

According to the Austrailian Border Force, a joint operation between the Australian Border Force (ABF) and the Australian Federal Police (AFP), in cooperation with the US Department of Homeland Security Investigations (HSI), New Zealand Customs Service (NZCS) and the Canada Border Services Agency (CBSA) has resulted in the seizure of approximately 95 kilograms of cocaine from a Cruise Ship in Sydney.

The police also announced the arrest of three Canadian nationals on drug importation charges.

Police reported that on Sunday, August 28, 2016, ABF officers boarded the Sea Princess when it berthed in Sydney Harbour, and with the assistance of detector dogs, searched some passenger cabins on the ship. During this search, approximately 95 kilograms of cocaine was located, packed in suitcases belonging to those arrested.

AFP officers report that they then arrested the three Canadian nationals, a 63-year-old man, a 28-year-old woman, and a 23-year old woman.

All three appeared in Sydney Central Local Court on Monday, Aug. 29, 2016, charged with importing a commercial quantity of cocaine.

The maximum penalty for this offense is life imprisonment.

ABF Assistant Commissioner, Strategic Border Command, Clive Murray said that this was yet another example of international cooperation leading to significant results in the fight against international drug syndicates.

"These syndicates should be on notice that the Australian Border Force is aware of all of the different ways they attempt to smuggle drugs into our country and we are working with a range of international agencies to stop them," Assistant Commissioner Murray said.

Chapter Eight

Take a cheap January Cruise

(Note: These prices existed for sailings in 2016. They are typical prices for cruises shopped for and purchased under similar circumstances using these tips.)

Okay, the snow and ice started piling up on the driveway, the forecast was for even more for the next two months as you sit around the week after Christmas wishing that you had shopped for a cruise sometime next month to take you to the Caribbean.

Well, good news, Pilgrim!

The cruise companies have lots of ships, some new, some old and some blue, just waiting for you!

All you have to do is hit Google and spin the pages and land on a DEAL!

How about $199?

Doing exactly as outlined above, the first to come up on the first page of Google is Priceline, scrolling down the page a 4-night stay in the crime-ridden Bahamas on the Norwegian Sky is available from Miami to Freeport, Nassau, Great Stirrup Cay (the private island of NCL and back to Miami. The interior room works out to $50 a night and the ship will be packed with drunks as your room (double occupancy) includes the Complimentary Ultimate Beverage Package. Attempting to book passage on the Jan. 4, 2016 bargain price of $449 the website rolls over to a pink bar with a message to call an 800 number to continue booking your cruise – likely due to the cruise leaving in under ten days. This is the bottom price for this ship of tools, who will all attempt to get every last drop of alcohol that they can on the trip. If you like to have a little cruise in your quest for rum, this is the cruise for you. For teetotalers, find another ship, you likely will not be happy.

CRUISE FACTS

Complimentary Ultimate Beverage Package Included

From the NCL website: Call to book any stateroom category on select Norwegian Sky sailings and receive an ultimate beverage package. This offer is valid for all clients traveling in the same stateroom. Guests must be at least 21 years of age at the time of sailing to qualify. Guests 3 to 20 years of age will receive a soda package. Ultimate Beverage Package includes a wide variety of premium spirits and cocktails, wines by the glass and bottle or draft beer up to $11 per serving. Non-alcoholic beer is also included. This is a personal package; only one beverage per guests will be served. Room service and mini-bar are not included. Additional restrictions may apply. Please call to book and for more information.

Should you live in Miami or South Florida and someone will drop you off at the ship eliminating the need for parking or taxis, this is a great deal.

How about those who live within a five-hour drive of New York and are interested in spending two weeks in the Caribbean, don't want to fly to Florida and have to run into all those from the Northeast, who live there in the winter. You just want to get on a boat with your bags that stay packed and start having someone wait on you hand and foot.

NCL has a new ship that they homeport in New York City, the Breakaway. A cheap rate is to be had for an Inside cabin from $799 for sailings on Jan. 3 and Jan. 17, the prices are higher for February sailings. The price in February is $1,049 per person for an inside cabin, but if the ship fails to fill as the Jan. 31 and Feb. 14 sailings near, the price will likely drop again. There is a lot to be said for working your computer on a daily basis. An ocean view room is available for $100 more, but you will see all the ocean you want every day without having to sit around your room. Take the inside cabin as whenever you are in the room; it is dark outside anyway.

This is an example of how to identify and book a cheap cruise, without the use of an agent. Agents are knowledgeable and building a relationship with the same agent over a period can pay off as well. In today's era of internet booking, it is possible and easy for you to find what you want, the deal you like, and then call the cruise line directly to book or call an agent and tell them what you want.

The option of finding last minute deals in the middle of winter, especially during the somewhat off month of January is great.

Where is the Breakaway going for that $799 per person? It really doesn't matter. Some islands are better than others. Any is great. Keep your wits about you both on the ship and on shore. Remember the issues of crime on ships and ports are more thoroughly examined in other chapters of this book.

The Breakaway trip for Jan. 3rd and Jan. 17th are especially a good choice in that the first two days are at sea, the next two stops at San Juan and St. Thomas, both of which are beautiful.

However, both contain criminals who excel at avoiding punishment due to the fact both are United States territories but run by politicians who are on par with any big city corrupt officials on the mainland. In San Juan stick to a tour or stay in the Old San Juan and don't wander off the beaten track. Same in St. Thomas.

The bright spot on this trip is that this ship stops at St. Maarten, British Virgin Island Tortola (the criminals are not coddled) and Dominica, Barbados, and Martinique, finishing with a stop at Antiqua where criminals again are dangerous and fairly aggressive.

All in all, this is a terrific itinerary at a great price on a new ship. Even with four sea days, you are still spared flying, and Academy bus can take the pain out of parking.

Norwegian also has last minute deals on other itineraries. The Pride of America tours seven nights and days in Hawaii with a "brochure" price of $4,019 and rates for $1,399 and up.

Cruises Only is a dependable cruise travel agency which has served me well for years. They offer the $1399 deal for January sailings for the seven-night voyage as well as an 11 night Hawaii from San Francisco for $1899, both for inside cabins. Thus, the air would be R/T from your city to San Francisco, and residents of the region on the West Coast will have much lower costs to arrive at the dock to embark on the cruise and to return home. Upgrades and special offers are also available for limited times.

CRUISE FACTS

As in the chapter on last-minute air deals for trans-Atlantic cruises, a last minute air search for the Hawaii trip reveals: your last minute airfare round-trip for two seniors will cost from $873 to $901 with American, United, Alaska and Delta. All range from 16 hours to 22 hours due mainly to the fact that the islands are on the other side of the world, and most fares require two stops to take on fuel and passengers.

PHOTO: Not walking on the railings is a good way to avoid this view of a cruise ship. The Holland America Amsterdam at anchor in the Bahamas. THE PRIVATEER CLAUSE photo

On my last flight to Hawaii to meet the Holland America Zaandam to give maritime history talks, I spent another $65 on an upgrade to business class over the basic coach provided for me by the cruise line and it was a smart thing to do for the long ride.

Therefore, with $2400 per person for a roundtrip flight from airports in the Washington DC area to Hawaii, a seven-day cruise; this a great trip for a reasonable price. Many similar trips on other ships are available, and it's entirely possible you will find a better deal than I found in just a few minutes.

KEN ROSSIGNOL
Spring Special:

A 9 Night Baltic Capitals voyage on the Norwegian Star departs from Copenhagen. The cruise leaves on May 8th thus the search of Tripadvisor.com reveals round-trip air for two from Baltimore on Wow Air at $598 per person. Other resulted included flight and hotel package which could come in handy for spending several days before and after your cruise in Copenhagen. Results from Expedia show rates of $750 and up per person roundtrip on Iceland Air and Turkish Airlines. Non-stop service is available at about $880.

The price of cruise: Inside cabin from $1214, R/T air $600 equals a basic price of $1800 per person before taxis, tours, tips and hotel stay at each end of the cruise. All in all, a frugal spender can do this trip for $2,500 each for a couple.

The Norwegian Epic at port in Miami. THE PRIVATEER CLAUSE photo

The Norwegian Star in port in Bermuda at the Royal Dockyard.
THE PRIVATEER CLAUSE photo

The Norwegian Dawn passes under the Verrazano Bridge in New York.
THE PRIVATEER CLAUSE photo

Cruise lines host some of the most intense collections of art on their ships. This painting is on the **Celebrity Eclipse.** THE PRIVATEER CLAUSE photo

Chapter Nine

Do you want a slice of lemon with that Caribbean Crime?

Samana marketplace in the Dominican Republic. THE PRIVATEER CLAUSE photo

The first time I visited the Dominican Republic was on an old classic ocean liner in 1985. This was just about the time the modern cruise lines were cranking up, and when we visited one Caribbean port, everyone was excited to see the huge Norway, anchored nearby. Even that long ago, the word was passed among passengers about crime in the ports we visited.

KEN ROSSIGNOL

It is rare for a ship to dock today in the Dominican Republic but some do. Walking to a nearby "tourist village" is about as adventuresome as a cruise passenger should be, though some water-oriented tours are safe, or, at least, safer than venturing off by yourself or with one or two others.

Fishing boats in the harbor of Samana, Dominican Republic. THE PRIVATEER CLAUSE photo

Common sense can be a foreign word to many travelers, and the lack thereof can be the source of most incidents of passengers becoming crime victims. However, the complicity of the cruise lines cannot be ignored.

When our ship arrived at Puerto Plato, we took note of the fact that the lines for disembarking were small and that most of the passengers stayed on the ship. That was because they were veteran cruisers and had common sense. We were young and dumb. And lucky.

CRUISE FACTS

A Virgin Island's Police cruiser is a welcome sight in St. Thomas. THE PRIVATEER CLAUSE photo

From the cruise terminal to the town it was a walk of about a mile. Every hundred feet or so was a soldier with a machine gun. That should have been the first clue. Turn around and run for the ship.

We didn't. We kept on walking with the 'shop till you drop' mantra and the gleam in the eyes of the womenfolk yearning to be freed of their cash in exchange for "deals" on jewelry overpowering all common sense.

I counted the soldiers with each passing store front.

Finally, after a couple of jewelry stores and a few cold beers, the thirst for foreign adventures in shopping was quelled. Our return trip to the pier was peaceful. We had picked up a "guide" who walked along with his to assure our visit was a success. He didn't have a gun, and we weren't quite sure why he was with us.

The best way to get around in Bermuda is the public ferry and to a lesser extent, the bus system. *THE PRIVATEER CLAUSE photo*

Serenade of the Seas at the dock. THE PRIVATEER CLAUSE photo

At the gangplank, we offered our "guide" a gratuity of ten dollars. He said flatly that he charges $200 for such service as he provided. Since the cash had been depleted, except for the ten spot forked over to the guide, we looked at him and realized that he was the only robber we had met that day. Whether or not he provided any service beyond simply walking along with us was unknown to us at the time. It could be he actually might have prevented us from being mugged when we were among soldiers.

Criminals are opportunistic.

Stay with a group. Don't venture off by yourself in port. Older frail people are easy marks. A whistle and some pepper spray might save your life.

THE BOTTOM LINE: Don't be a sitting duck.

By all means travel, but don't wander into side streets where there are no cops or crowds.

The following is a report from a port where folks put themselves into harm's way. If you expect the cruise line to provide you with a stern warning about your port visit, you are expecting too much.

CRUISE FACTS

From CruiseLawNews.com

A couple of days ago, we posted an article about cruise passengers who were robbed while visiting the Altun Ha Maya Ruins site in Belize. During this incident, two cruise passengers were reportedly robbed of a gold necklace and $450 in cash by two men, one with a machete and one with a handgun.

A local television station said that "the tourism police officers were lax in carrying out their duties. When the last tourist bus left, so did the tourism police, although the site had not been closed."

But the Ministry of Culture later issued a press release saying "there were adequate police and security presence at the Archeological Site."

Today, we were notified by a passenger, wishing to stay anonymous, who visited Belize City on a Royal Caribbean cruise ship, the Vision of the Seas, and told us that her husband had been physically assaulted and battered in an apparent robbery attempt on March 8th after their cruise ship docked at the Tourism Village. She indicated that after a ten-minute walk from the port on Gabourel Lane, she and her husband ate lunch and began to return to the ship. A local man "came up from behind with a rifle and said he was going to kill us if he did not get my bag." Here is her account:

"We were victims of an attempted armed robbery on Tuesday, March 8, 2016, near the Museum of Belize after lunch at Senor Coconuts while walking back to port. My husband was hit on the head with the barrel of a rifle and sustained an injury to the head (requiring stitches) and bruises on the arm and hand, and I also sustained scratches and bruises. Luckily, there was a woman nearby who scared him off. The police never arrived until we were at the hospital. We were driven there by a couple in the area. We were treated at the hospital and driven back to port. We were on RC Vision of the Seas. It is our understanding there is little police presence because they are underfunded and undermanned. This is a very dangerous place filled with crime and cruise ship visitors are not advised of this by the ships. I was really concerned because of all the young college girls on the ship. Do not go out of Tourism Village. The city of Belize is very unsafe."

The passenger told me "I want people to know if it weren't for two kind women, I don't know what more could have happened . . . There were three cruise ships in port that day, probably over 3,000 people. The cruise ships need to warn you, but they don't. We learned the hard way."

This view of the approach to the Royal Dockyard shows the advantage a lookout or gun crew would have on an approaching ship.
THE PRIVATEER CLAUSE photo

So much for the Fountain of Youth. This is the tomb of Ponce De Leon in the Cathedral in Old San Juan, Puerto Rico. THE PRIVATEER CLAUSE photo

CHAPTER TEN

At this point, you are likely ready to take a cruise you can afford, one where you will have fun, be aware of the dangers present on the ship and shore and return alive.

Information is power.

At this point, you should likely know that cruise line websites, travel company websites which include Cruise Critic, which is owned by a travel company website which earns its living from ads placed by cruise lines as well as commissions paid for booking passengers – are all propaganda sheets for the cruise line companies.

Major media sources of news coverage of cruise lines are simplistic with a few exceptions, and provide little to no context to issues of cruise travel. The major media outlets swoop in at a time of disaster, pluck the high ratings for a couple of days and leave.

One major exception was the 2016 event of the Anthem of The Seas which sailed directly into the path of a storm with hurricane force winds. The captain of the ship failed to remain in port and along with the corporate chiefs, allowed more than 6,000 souls to be endangered only for the purpose of adhering to a schedule.

The captain lied directly to his passengers when giving a sweetheart interview with his cruise director, which was broadcast on the ship TV system. The interview was videoed by a passenger who then posted it on YouTube, for the benefit of viewers to get first-hand, the incompetence of the captain and Royal Caribbean.

It appeared to me that when Royal Caribbean International allowed this sailing into the winter storm on the Atlantic, that Carnival must have bought out its competitor. That was not the case, but Royal showed at that moment that they were as idiotic as Carnival was when that firm allowed its customers to steam on a slow sewage cruise from just off the coast of Mexico, under tow to Mobile, Alabama, all for the purpose of saving on airfare.

When the Anthem captain and Royal officials tried to parse words and promote blatant lies, major media weather casters put the lie to their words with facts, charts and computer tracks of the storm along with the forecasts which were available at the time. In particular, NBC's Al Roker should be acknowledged, along with the Weather Channel for rebutting the lies of Royal Caribbean.

The Anthem should have stayed in port, but didn't. It sailed directly into the storm, something I had never would have believed Royal Caribbean would have ever allowed.

On Feb. 10, 2016, Royal Caribbean International issued this statement:
"We apologize for exposing our guests and crew to the weather they faced, and for what they went through.

Our ship and our crew performed very well to keep everyone safe during severe weather. Of more than 6000 people on board, only four minor injuries were reported.

Despite that fact, the event, exceptional as it was, identified gaps in our planning system that we are addressing. Though that system has performed well through many instances of severe weather around the world, what happened this week showed that we need to do better.

The severity of Sunday's storm, with its 120-mph winds, far exceeded forecasts. Even so, it is our responsibility to eliminate every surprise we possibly can.

As of today, we are strengthening our storm avoidance policy and have added resources at our Miami headquarters to provide additional guidance to our ships' captains.

CRUISE FACTS

As for Anthem of the Seas, much of the superficial damage caused by the storm has been repaired. We expect to resume her planned itinerary for next week's cruise.

Again, we offer our apologies to our guests and crew."

The above statement contained several lies, an apology and failed to identify any individual for responsibility. No one was fired.

The danger came when the ship lost one of its propulsion systems. The ship lost its ability to correctly maneuver and adjust to the wind direction, which was hitting at 100 mph.

News reports later tracked the progress of the ship back to port in New Jersey, but the major media lacked the expertise to realize that the slow trip back was due to the loss of one of the two main propulsion systems. The other was damaged as the ship heaved in and out of the water, with the giant propulsion pod spinning in the air.

Had the second pod failed completely, the ship would have been at the mercy of the wind. The towering decks catch a lot of wind and the reports from passengers about how the ship heaved and listed would never have been received as the Anthem would have capsized. At those angles, there would have been no point in launching lifeboats as the ship would have been incapable of doing so. Few passengers would have been rescued as most would have been trapped inside the ship in a scene reminiscent of the Poseidon movie.

Ships should not sail into the path of a storm; especially one with thousands of lives on board

Seamanship is not a theory; it is an art. One practiced and taken seriously by all masters of vessels of any size and anywhere in the world.

Predicting bad weather and storms is also not a theory but science, aided by the most sophisticated instruments and technology.

El Faro crew of 33 lost in hurricane due to Captain's decision to sail.

For Captains and companies to sail their ships into bad weather is foolhardy, dangerous and when someone is killed, criminally negligent.

When Hurricane Sandy was sweeping up the Atlantic in 2012, the storm was well forecast, there was no surprise at its power, it was not unexpected, yet the Captain of the tall ship Bounty sailed from a safe port into the storm, losing his life, injuring others and sinking the vessel.

The freighter El Faro that sailed from Jacksonville into the path of Hurricane Joaquin in 2015, causing the ship to sink with all thirty-three hands on board disappearing forever, was a direct result of corporate stupidity and cowardice on the part of the captain to fail to stand up for the lives of his crew. The National Transportation Safety Board will finalize its investigation in another year or so. However, the official cause will likely mirror what was widely apparent: a failure to heed a forecast of a hurricane.

Royal Caribbean's decision to adhere to a scheduled cruise from Bayonne, New Jersey to the Bahamas was again a case of a Captain failing to take a proper path out and around a forecasted major storm or stay in port until it passes.

Everything associated with a cruise is weather dependent and the cruise lines make it clear that ports will be missed should weather turn bad, itineraries will change, and plans will be turned upside down.

I was on the Celebrity Eclipse where the weather blew up in our intended route and the Captain wisely changed the port calls to different ports to avoid the worse of a late fall storm off the coast of France and Spain in 2011. It was a good thing he did, as while we skirted the storm, the seas were in were rough and dangerous. People were tossed, dishes scooted off tables and the adventure was in full drama. Not as bad as on the Anthem but enough to make one remember and appreciate that the Captain removed us to calmer waters.

To Royal Caribbean's credit, the cruise line immediately issued a notice to its customers that their fare would be refunded, and a future cruise would be half the cost of what they paid on the Anthem. Ironically, had the ship detoured out and around the storm or simply stayed in port for two days, the monetary loss would likely have been similar without the risk to life.

Why didn't the Anthem head for the nearest safe port in Charleston, S.C.?

As it was, the financial decision made by Royal Caribbean to sail directly into the path of a dangerous winter storm with forecast hurricane force winds was stupid, criminal and wanton. A disaster would have made the Costa Concordia look like a picnic and dwarfed the death toll on the Titanic.

CRUISE FACTS

Al Roker, the popular television weatherman on the Today Show, best summed up Royal Caribbean's claim that the storm was not predicted: **"Royal Caribbean's claim that this was not predicted is bull feathers. "**

Weather Expert Slams Royal Caribbean as Negligent

From NJ.com

The decision by Royal Caribbean to let one of its cruise ships head into the path of a powerful storm system swirling in the Atlantic Ocean this past weekend has not only come under attack by frightened passengers but also by a weather expert who was closely monitoring the development of the storm.

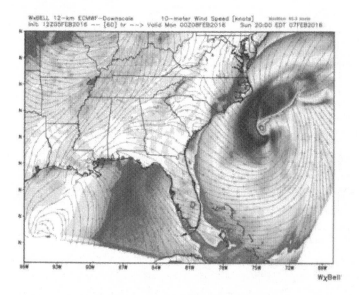

Ryan Maue, a digital meteorologist for WeatherBell Analytics, said it's hard to believe no one at Royal Caribbean had been aware of a storm system that had been forecast — and included in official advisories and warnings issued by the National Weather Service — days in advance.

"The storm was well forecast by many different weather models from every agency. This was not a surprise to anyone watching the weather on a daily basis," Maue said Monday afternoon. "The extreme impacts were also quite predictable and expected by meteorologists at NOAA OPC (the National Oceanic and

Atmospheric Administration's Ocean Prediction Center) and private forecasting companies. Folks all marveled at the extreme intensity of this storm on Twitter."

From Cruise Critic forum post by a passenger on Anthem:

"We are on the Anthem right now, left NY yesterday, we sailed in a storm that intensified very quickly, Captain tried to turn ship but waited too long. We have been stuck in 125+ mph winds 30+ foot waves for 4 hours. Captain said they are in communication with the coast guard, struggling to point ship into the wind but can't move forward. All passengers told to stay in cabins water entered the ship on upper decks, large white structure broke off the top of ship landed in the pool. At the height of storm waves breaking above the top of lifeboats and ship listing almost 45 degrees, with the wind looked like a total white out. Conditions are improving but damage all over the ship, the crew looked concerned and sounded very concerned on the intercom. Some passengers are sitting in muster stations. "

GCaptain reported: "The Coast Guard says it did not receive a distress call from the Anthem of the Seas but contacted the ship after seeing posts on Twitter and social media."

One Voice Against the Industry Slant

One of the few independent sources of news of cruise travel is the website of Miami lawyer Jim Walker, on his Cruiselaw.com.

The cruise lines would likely challenge Walker as being independent as he represents those who wish to litigate against the cruise lines.

The purpose of this book is not to evaluate either position but instead to advocate for your knowledge in cruise travel.

In this day and age of corporations such as the major cruise lines being deceptive to their customers, governments around the world being corrupt and incompetent, and terrorist groups all wanting to kill you in the name of Islamic fanatic goals, the ability to have a safe and fun vacation is severely challenged.

Gone are the days of traveling by ship safely on the Mediterranean. Islamic terrorists blew up a ferry off of the Philippines, killing 124 people. Terrorists attacked passengers from cruise ships at Tunis, killing many of them.

Bookings in Europe on ships are sagging forcing the CEO's of Norwegian and Royal Caribbean to make personal buys of their company stock in publicity stunts.

Still – cruise travel remains the safest way to travel around the world and presents the best value as well.

Hamilton harbor hosts the ferry terminal which transports local commuters and tourists to the Royal Dockyard at the other end of the island. *THE PRIVATEER CLAUSE photo*

CHAPTER ELEVEN

Congratulations. You made it this far. Now let's go through a checklist on how to cruise cheap, fun and safe.

First – let's save money.

Book in advance and pick the cruise you want to take but at the same time, get for the best price available. Remember, no ship is leaving the dock with empty rooms. Those who booked six months to a year in advance are more likely to pay the advertised initial rates. Those who book in the last thirty days are going to get the bargains.

But how do you get both the cruise you want, the cabin you want and yet get the bargain rate?

Go ahead and use a major travel company online but check the rates for the cruise you book every day.

Why?

Because the world economy tosses up such things as wars, civil unrest, bank failures and sunspots that cause all manner of disruptions to fares.

Mayhem in the Med causes passengers to cancel and forces cruise lines to cancel port visits to places where heads are rolling, and tourists are being machine-gunned in a museum such as took place in Tunis. What that means is that ships are going to be diverted to another location.

This is all about supply and demand. Increase the number of ships to the sunny Caribbean by reducing ships working the fall season in the Med, as is taking place now, and it makes the remaining cruises in the Med higher as those seeking such a voyage have fewer choices. The prices for a Med cruise will go up. The prices in the Caribbean will become more competitive.

The half dozen ships sent to work the Caribbean three months early translates into sudden great deals on Trans-Atlantic trips when those are already booked for that ship can't adjust their schedule and get moved to another ship. The revolving door of re-bookings might go on forever, but in every instance, the cruise lines are going to be doing their best to make customers happy when they are rebooked. This is the time to ask for incentives. Free gratuities, free beverage packages, free excursions, discount on future cruises or anything you might imagine. This is the time to be creative.

After all, it's not your fault the King of Siam got iced by his brother or Ahab decided to overthrow the Potentate Extraordinaire of The Nile.

CRUISE FACTS

But the cruise line who wants you to move to another cruise on the same ship or a different ship or simply to another cabin will be amenable to your request such as: "...this would make me happy if you would..."

You may be very surprised at the answer.

Remember, these floating hotels can bring hundreds of extra rooms to a port on short notice. The law of supply and demand will be reflected in the email blasts that end up in your inbox on a daily basis promising BLOWOUT PRICES ON LAST MINUTE CRUISES!!!

Those email blasts are also used by travel companies to get rid of a block of rooms that they had committed to filling on a ship. They essentially are dumping their excess unsold inventory for any price, even below the advertised prices you see on the internet.

A CLUE:

Those last minute deals will have the words CALL FOR PRICE. Make the call and have your credit card ready to buy as these generally are only good that day. You don't have to be pushed into buying and can easily take a pass if you have a flexible schedule.

In that case, keep shopping.

UPGRADES:

For those who booked early, just do a daily simple Google check for prices on the ship and voyage on which you are booked. If you see a cheaper rate, this is the time to bug your travel agent or the cruise line if you booked directly with them. This method is how to get an upgrade.

They don't really want to match the price at the current advertised rates and will point to language in your contract that says they don't have to.

However, they do want to keep you happy and may say,' given your loyalty to the XYZ Cruise Company, I can upgrade you to a Balcony!'

Now you have gone from an ocean view to a balcony which can easily run $400 per person higher, depending on the ship, the cruise and the market.

PORT MONEY SAVERS – Skip the ship tours completely. Dream up your own tour and booking an Uber driver for an impromptu last-minute tour of the Old Panama City like we did last month gave us an hour-long tour in a nice sedan with no other passengers, stopping wherever we wanted, and an agreeable driver, all charged to our Uber account that rang up to a total of $38 including tip. No cash or credit cards change hands with Uber. You determine you own tipping percentage when you set up your account.

When we had seen enough of this really nice historic district, we went out and did the shopping gig on foot and then had dinner at Las Clementina's, which has a 4.5-star rating on Trip Advisor, and then called for another Uber for a trip back to our hotel. The restaurant provided us with an exceptional dinner for less than $40 total.

A typical tour of a port city could run more than $50 each if booked through a ship. The cruise line tries to scare you into booking with them with baloney such as they screen the tour operators; they won't leave you behind and so forth. If you decide to take tour an hour before the ship leaves, you deserve to be left behind.

BOOK YOUR TOUR IN ADVANCE

This method has its perils as ports can change at the last minute and cause havoc to your booked tour with an agency like Spain Day Tours like we used in Spain on several cruises. They are excellent. They also stay abreast of port changes due to weather and will shift their assets to the new port, and you may never realize the difference. You likely won't miss your trip to the winery and won't remember the visit anyway after consuming five glasses of wine.

Look on the Cruise Critic Boards and watch for someone trying to add more people to their booked tour in a small van. The big bus can be just fine or be a pain as some old biddies won't stop shopping and get their big packages back to the bus at the appointed time. This is a good time to take a nap or a nip out of one of the bottles you picked up at the winery.

Be careful if you are the tour organizer and have paid in advance. The wonderful folks who joined your tour might give your group the slip when it is time to pay up. Get the money before you leave the parking lot for the tour. One nice fellow from Florida told folks they could pay him at the end of a tour to the Normandy beaches but disappeared when we got back to Cherbourg, and he had to pay the driver for the two who vanished.

WALK OR TAKE A BUS TO A BEACH

If you can't figure out how to get to a popular beach without a ship tour, then you will just have to pay more for not overcoming your fear of the internet. Learn how to use the internet. Your grandchildren use it and if you are honest about life, you know, deep in your heart, you are just as smart or smarter than your grandchildren and a heck of a lot smarter than your children. On an island such as St. Kitts or Antiqua, and most others, there are resorts nearby who may give you a sweet deal on their grounds for a few hours, including lunch, a few drinks and nice chairs and umbrellas for a cheap fee. A cab or Uber gets you there, and there may be a public bus.

In Bermuda, many have found the public bus ride to Horseshoe Beach to be great, and another beach is within walking distance of the Royal Dockyard. There is a great museum there as well in addition to The Frog and Onion Pub. Get the $20 or so person ferry-bus pass for your stay in Bermuda and take the bus once as it's a heckuva ride, and the ferries are one of the best values and nicest experiences you will find in any port. Also, Bermuda really treats folks nicely; it is clean, well-ordered and a bit pricey. The bus and ferry personnel are excellent in every way. Polite to a fault. A cheap Wi-Fi pass for 24 hours is a good way to check in and avoid the lousy and expensive Wi-Fi on your ship. Go over to the gift shop in the square at the Royal Dockyard; there are big signs. Buy it there. It will even work on the promenade deck of your ship as you are in port for the night.

If you bought the ship Wi-Fi package and it is slow, go to the front desk and complain. They likely will remove the charge from your bill but leave the line open so you can continue to use the slow service. But, get off your device and have fun.

A trip that includes Bermuda, or is the sole destination, will be one you will savor.

PORT DAYS – Stay on board.

Most ships will offer great deals on a massage or other services in the spa on a port day as less of their audience will be in captivity. They can't make any money off of the folks out on tours or who have wisely taken a public bus to a beach.

There are far fewer people on the ship in the port to pee in the pool or cause lines at the ice cream machine. The hot tubs will have fewer people stew cooking as well. Consider avoiding the hot tubs.

Just consider the bacteria are cooking in that water when it splashes in your mouth. They used to put missionaries in such heated cauldrons in the jungle.

Then there is the joke about the two missionaries being boiled alive by natives and one is smiling. The other one says, "what gives, why are you smiling?" The first one answers, "I just seasoned their stew!"

All over the world, in every port, is free air-conditioning and a place to sit. God likes visitors, too.

Veteran cruisers will walk around the port shops for a bit and then return to the ship for empty decks and pools, all to themselves. First timers to St. Martin's will head to the nude beach on the French side. There are legal brothels in St. Maarten on the Dutch side and Secret Service rates apply.

When going ashore:
1. Leave your bling behind. There is little sense in trolling for criminals.
2. Have the phone number of the ship on your phone?
3. Have your photo ID and copy of your passport at all times. Best to have your passport and keep the photocopy in your cabin safe.
4. If you do not have common sense, hang around with someone who does, it will come in handy.

5. Stay in crowds, don't go waltzing down an empty side street unless you are packing heat.
6. You are an official American or Western tourist bringing criminals a feast. These Dirtbags make their living off of stealing and mugging. Don't expect them to work for a living. They make their girlfriends hold down jobs. You are their reward for being clever.
7. U.S. Virgin Islands and Puerto Rico, Hawaii and Alaska are local calls for U.S. residents; check with your service provider in advance to verify this and to add on international calling.
8. *The Murder Rate in the U.S. Virgin Islands* is the highest in all the nation and its territories. When you get off the ship it is like you are entering into a criminal zone in U.S. cities you would never visit. According to CruiseLawNews.com, "The territory has a staggering homicide rate around 35.5 per 100,000 people, whereas the United States as a whole has a rate around 4.7 per 100,000 people. (In 2012, the per capita murder rate in the USVI was even higher, around 56 per 100,000 people)."

SHIP CRIME

1. Your ship likely has its share of thieves and con-men just like the hometown you left behind. Some will be crew, and some will be your fellow passengers.
2. Lock up your good stuff in your cabin safe.
3. Don't leave pricey stuff on your deck chair while you hop over to the bar, have a good time in the line dancing or hang around the pool grill. It will walk.
4. Imbibe in moderation.
5. Stay off the railings. No one "falls overboard" even though the morons in the media always reports those words. Sharks have to eat too, and there is no sense in ruining the fun for everyone by doing a search.
6. Always have a pocket flashlight in your pocket or purse.

WHATSAPP

Sign up with this outfit before leaving home and you can talk free with anyone of your contacts who also have the App, as well as a text for free. From their website: "With WhatsApp, you'll get fast, simple, secure messaging and calling for free*, available on phones all over the world."

WI-FI

Royal Caribbean's new VOOM internet service has changed the way you will think about the old clunky Wi-Fi at sea.

FROM ROYAL CARIBBEAN:

Here are the exclusive package features:

The SURF package will let you browse the web, stay in touch via email, and share vacation photos on social media. Starting at $19.99 per device, additional devices can be added at a discounted cost.

The SURF AND STREAM package provide all the access to the SURF package, as well as the capability to stream movies and music from Netflix and Spotify, and video chat with apps like Skype. This package is available for $27.99 per device, and additional devices also can be connected at a discount (note: pricing is subject to change).

FIRST DAY ON THE SHIP

1. Avoid the buffet area where it is a madhouse and check out the alternative venues which most passengers won't know exist because they follow the feeding frenzy to the Golden Corral on board – many times called the Windjammer.
2. Beware of room service. On many lines, morning breakfast and late night snacks now carry a fee. Have your room attendant pack up your minibar and check your bill every day for items added to your bill that you didn't consume. Cruise line personnel make mistakes and are quick to fix them. They really want your business and to have you enjoy your trip and return again soon. Be sure to tip your room service waiter.
3. Some of the fee-based specialty restaurants on ships are now open for breakfast and Norwegian offers great omelets in the O'Sheehan's. Celebrity offers breakfast in Bistro on Five. Check your daily newsletter for venues and hours.
4. Don't assume all the food items at the specialty coffee shops on ships are fee-based, much of the food is free.
5. Ice cream cones and cups are available at most buffets and ice cream machines are on many pool decks. The specialty

ice cream and gelato bars on Celebrity and other lines charge a fee.

6. Don't stand in line for a main dining room seat on the first night; it's a good night to go to a specialty restaurant, and if you check your program for the day, it may be there is a significant discount for that first day.

7. Order what you please at the main dining room. Want to try an entrée but not sure it's for you? Get the waiter to bring you an appetizer-sized portion of that entrée. Can't decide which appetizer to order? Order them both. Get as many desserts as you like. This is your vacation and the time to try new foods and meet new friends. And there is no charge for the extra sampling or bunches of entrees.

8. Like the fresh fruit in your stateroom? Pick up a plate full of fruit from the buffet and take it back to your cabin along with a plate of chocolate chip cookies.

9. There are those who buy the ship's brand of large water bottles to take ashore. They then stop at the cheap port liquor store and buy clear booze like vodka or gin, empty the water and pour the booze in the water bottle. Unless the ship security opens your bottle to take a whiff, they will let your 'water' bottle sail through the machine, and you will save a bit on your bar bill.

10. If you are a drinker, the drink packages available will have you tossing 'em down to get your money's worth. You won't remember too much of this cruise. Feel free to take your drink from one venue to another. Nobody cares.

11. Cruise line policies on what beverages you can bring on board varies and changes are in the wind:
Norwegian updated their policy effective July 15, 2016: "Effective for sailings July 15, 2016 and beyond, guests are prohibited from bringing any beverages -- including liquor, beer and non-alcoholic drinks such as water, soda and juices -- on board either as carry-on or checked luggage, with the exception of purified or distilled water in factory-sealed containers for use in conjunction with medical devices or for the reconstitution of infant formula; and fully sealed and/or corked wine bottles for personal consumption onboard that is subject to screening and a corkage fee (for guests 21 years of age or older). Open beverages of any kind must be consumed or discarded at

the security check-point, on embarkation day and at any port of call. This revised policy brings the company in line with other best practice travel security protocols and reduces the need for individual time-consuming screening and package inspection of large volumes of beverages."

12. Forget the soda package. It was too much money, and the iced tea, hot tea, coffee and watered down weird drinks in the buffet are free.
13. Turn your TV to the bridge cam at night in your cabin for a night light. Bring your own charging station or power strip for all your electronic gear as most staterooms have only a couple of electric outlets.
14. Most cruise lines will allow you to ask your room attendant to bring you an egg crate mattress topper which will put more space between you and the sweaty occupants who slept there before you.

Have a safe and fun voyage!

GET A FREE BOOK!

Visit ThePrivateerClause.com

59264739R00050

Made in the USA
Lexington, KY
30 December 2016